spicy
sichuan
cooking

Daniel Reid

This collection of over 30 Sichuan recipes includes all-time favorites such as Gung Bao Chicken, Ma Po Tofu, and Hot andSour Soup. With clear, easy-to-follow instructions and stunning photographs, *Spicy Sichuan Cooking* enables you to reproduce the hot and spicy flavors of the Sichuan kitchen at home.

PERIPLUS

Basic Ingredients

Dried red chilies

Fresh finger-
length chilies

Chilies are indispensable in Sichuanese cooking. The commonly-used red and green **finger-length chilies** are moderately hot. **Dried chilies** are usually cut in lengths and soaked in warm water to soften before use.

Chili oil is made from dried chilies or chili powder steeped in oil, and is used to flavor some Sichuan dishes. Bottled chili oil is also available in Asian markets.

Chili paste consists of ground fresh chilies, sometimes mixed with other ingredients such as vinegar, garlic or black beans, and commonly sold in jars. You may make your own and store it in the refrigerator, or purchase ready-made chili paste in Asian markets and well-stocked supermarkets.

Dried black Chinese mushrooms are used widely in Asian cooking. They are easily available from the dry food sections in wet markets and supermarkets. They must be soaked in hot water to soften before use. The stems are removed and discarded; only the caps are used. Dry or fresh shiitake mushrooms are a good substitute.

Dried prawns are tiny, orange prawns that have been dried in the sun. They come in different sizes. Available in Asian markets, they should look orangy-pink and plump; avoid any with a grayish appearance or an unpleasant smell. Dried prawns will keep for several months.

Fermented bean paste (*tau cheo* or *dou ban jiang*) is a richly-flavored seasoning made from soybeans, similar to Japanese miso (which may be used as a substitute). The beans are fermented and salted and sold in jars. They vary in color from dark brown to light golden. The basic fermented bean paste contains only soybeans, water and salt. It is

also possible to buy slightly sweetened versions or those with added chili. The beans are usually mashed with the back of a spoon before use.

Rice wine is used frequently in Chinese cooking. The best wine for Chinese cooking is *hua diao* rice wine, Japanese *sake* or *mirin*. A good alternative is dry sherry.

Sesame oil is pressed from sesame seeds that have been toasted, producing a dense and highly aromatic oil that can be used for cooking, marinades, sauces and soups, or as a table condiment. Its nutty, smokey flavor has become a hallmark of Chinese cuisine.

Sesame paste is made from ground, roasted sesame seeds and comes covered with oil in glass jars. It is quite hard and needs to be mixed with a little sesame oil or water to make it into a smooth paste. If you can't find it, use Middle Eastern tahini mixed with some sesame oil to give it a more pronounced flavor. Not to be confused with the sweet sesame paste made from black sesame seeds which is used in some snacks and desserts.

Sichuan peppercorns, also known as Chinese pepper or flower pepper (*hua jiao* in Mandarin) have a sharp pungency that tingles and slightly numbs the lips and tongue, an effect known in Chinese as *ma la* "numb hot."

Sichuan pepper-salt powder may be prepared by roasting 2 tablespoons Sichuan peppercorns in a dry pan with 1 teaspoon of sea salt, then grinding them to a fine powder. This makes an excellent table condiment.

Vinegar is used to balance flavors in sauces and to bring out the natural tastes of foods, almost always in conjunction with a bit of sugar; unless the recipe calls for a specific variety of Chinese vinegar, the best choices are rice vinegar or apple cider vinegar; red wine vinegars do not go well with Chinese food.

Wood ear fungus, is a thin, crinkly mushroom added to dishes for its crunchy texture. It is available both fresh and dried. Wash well and discard any hard patch in the center. Soak dried wood ear fungus in water until soft before using.

Soft tofu   Firm tofu

Tofu is rich in protein and amazingly versatile. **Silken** or **soft tofu** has a very fine texture, high water content and tends to break easily. **Firm tofu** holds its shape better when cut or cooked and has a stronger, slightly sour taste.

Regular Soy Sauce   Black Soy Sauce   Sweet Black Soy Sauce

Soy sauce is brewed from soybeans and wheat fermented with salt. It is salty and used as a table condiment and cooking seasoning. **Regular soy sauce** is a light clear brown liquid with a salty taste. **Black soy sauce** is denser, less salty and adds a smoky flavor to dishes. **Sweet black soy sauce** is a thick, fragrant sauce used in marinades and sauces

Pork and Prawn Dumplings with Chili Oil and Sichuan Pepper

250 g (8 oz) minced pork
250 g (8 oz) fresh prawns, peeled and finely chopped
4 spring onions, finely chopped
1 egg
2 tablespoons cornflour
2 teaspoons soy sauce
1 tablespoon minced or grated ginger
24 fresh or frozen round *wonton* wrappers
2 red finger-length chilies, sliced
2 tablespoons chopped fresh coriander leaves,

Sauce
3 teaspoons red chili oil
1 teaspoon sugar
1 teaspoon soy sauce
$1/2$ teaspoon salt
1 teaspoon Sichuan pep-percorn powder

1 Combine the Sauce ingredients in a small bowl, mix well and set aside.

2 To make the dumplings, combine the pork, chopped prawns, spring onions, egg, cornflour, soy sauce and ginger in a medium bowl and mix well.

3 Arrange several wrappers on a dry work surface and place a tablespoon of mixture onto the center of each wrapper. Using a pastry brush, lightly dab some water around half of the edge of the wrapper. Fold the wrapper in half and press the edges to seal. If not cooking immediately, lightly dust the dumplings and leave on a rack to dry without touching each other.

4 Bring a large pot of water to a rolling boil. Slip the dumplings into the boiling water, and let them boil until they all float to the surface, which means they are cooked. Remove from the water with a slotted spoon and drain.

5 Place the hot dumplings in a serving dish, pour the sauce and stir gently to coat. Alternatively, serve the sauce separately as a dip. Garnish with the sliced chili and coriander leaves and serve immediately.

Serves 4
Preparation time: **30 mins**
Cooking time: **5 mins**

Place a tablespoon of filling onto the center of each wrapper.

Lightly dab some water around half the edge, fold the wrapper in half and press the edges to seal.

Fish Soup with Sesame and Fennel

This recipe provides a variety of therapeutic benefits, including eliminating phlegm from the body, strengthening spleen and stomach functions, and counteracting symptoms of colds and flu. Any type of white-fleshed fish may be used in this soup.

500 g (1 lb) fresh white-fleshed fish, such as sea bass or swordfish
2 tablespoons sesame seeds, dry roasted, then finely ground in a blender or food processor
2 tablespoons oil
1$^1/_2$ liters (6 cups) boiling water or fish stock (made from fish bouillon cubes)
1 baby fennel bulb, halved, cored and finely sliced, leaves reserved to garnish

Seasoning
1 teaspoon soy sauce
1 teaspoon sugar
2 teaspoons fennel powder
1 teaspoon salt

1 Rinse the fish and pat dry with paper towels, then cut into bite-sized pieces.
2 Place the ground sesame seeds in a shallow bowl, then toss the fish pieces in the sesame powder until evenly coated. Cover the bowl and allow the fish to rest in the sesame powder for about 2 hours.
3 Combine the Seasoning ingredients and set aside.
4 Heat the oil in a wok or large pot until hot and stir-fry the fish for 2 minutes, then immediately add the boiling water or fish stock. Return to the boil, then add the Seasoning and stir to mix.
5 Cover, reduce the heat, and simmer for 5 minutes. Serve garnished with fennel slices and leaves if desired.

You may also prepare this soup with fresh prawns that have been shelled and deveined. This is a good way to prepare fish or prawns for people with digestive problems; the fennel and sesame aid digestion, and the water provides plenty of fluid to carry it through the digestive tract.

Fennel bulbs are stumpy plants with thick stems. They have round bases that resemble large onions and have an aniseed taste. They are sold fresh in supermarkets. If fennel bulbs are not available, substitute parsley.

Serves 4
Preparation time: **20 mins**
Marinating time: **2 hours**
Cooking time: **10 mins**

Clear Pork Soup with Daikon

Pork is a very popular meat in Sichuan and this is a favorite way to use pork to prepare soup. The preferred cut for this soup is what the Chinese call *wu hua rou*—literally "five flowered flesh"—which refers to the belly meat, or bacon cut, with its flowery pattern of fat and flesh. Leaner cuts may also be used. This is also a good example of how the famous Sichuan peppercorn can wake up an otherwise sleepy soup with its pungent flavor.

1 liter (4 cups) water, or chicken or vegetable stock (made from chicken or vegetable bouillon cubes)
4 slices ginger
2 spring onions, each cut into 3 sections
10 Sichuan peppercorns
1 daikon radish (about 250 g/8 oz), halved lengthwise, and sliced
300 g (10 oz) pork belly or bacon pork, or other tender cut, washed and cut into very thin slices

Sauce
2 teaspoons salt
1 teaspoon sugar
$1/2$ teaspoon freshly ground black pepper
2 teaspoons rice wine
2 teaspoons sesame oil

1 Mix the Sauce ingredients well and set aside.
2 Bring the chicken or vegetable stock or water to a boil in a pot, and add the ginger, spring onions and peppercorns. Add the Sauce and daikon slices, and stir. Lower the heat to medium and simmer, covered, for 12 minutes.
3 Add the pork, stir, cover again, and simmer for 3 more minutes, then turn off the heat completely.
4 Before serving, discard the ginger and spring onions. Transfer the soup to a soup bowl to serve at the table, or ladle individual servings into bowls.

This soup may also be prepared with beef or lamb. The best choice from the point of view of health is lamb, because lamb fat is far more digestible and actually benefits the human liver and heart, rather than clogging them up. You may also try using fresh fish fillets cut into thin strips, in which case you should reduce the final cooking time (when fish is added to the soup) to only 1 minute. Fresh chopped coriander leaves or parsley may be sprinkled onto each individual serving as a garnish.

Serves 4
Preparation time: **15 mins**
Cooking time: **20 mins**

Hot and Sour Soup

There are many ways of preparing the famous Sichuan hot and sour soup. Heavily seasoned and chock-full of highly nutritious ingredients, it is particularly popular as a winter food. The recipe given here includes various meat ingredients, but an equally tasty vegetarian version may also be prepared (see note below).

100 g (4 oz) chicken breast
30 g (1 oz) Yunnan ham or prosciutto
1 cake firm tofu
30 g (1 oz) canned or fresh bamboo shoots (see note)
1 small carrot
4 big fresh or dried black Chinese mushrooms
30 g (1 oz) wood ear mushrooms
1 liter (4 cups) chicken or vegetable stock, or plain water
2 teaspoons salt
1 teaspoon sugar
75 g ($^1/_2$ cup) green peas
2 eggs, well beaten
1$^1/_2$ tablespoons soy sauce
2 tablespoons vinegar
2 teaspoons sesame oil
$^1/_2$ teaspoon freshly ground black pepper
$^1/_2$ teaspoon Sichuan peppercorn powder
2 tablespoons cornflour mixed with 4 tablespoons cool water
1 bunch fresh coriander leaves, chopped
6 slices ginger, finely shredded
4 spring onions, chopped

Serves 4
Preparation time: 30 mins
Cooking time: 30 mins

1 Poach the chicken and ham in boiling water for 2 minutes, then drain and set aside to cool. Shred finely with fingers or a sharp knife and set aside.
2 Cut the firm tofu, bamboo shoots, and carrot, and set aside.
3 If using dried mushrooms, soak them separately in hot water for 20 minutes and drain. Diced all the mushrooms, discarding the stems, and set aside.
4 Bring the chicken or vegetable stock to a boil in a large pot. Add the salt, sugar, peas and the reserved meat and vegetables and stir well. Return to the boil, reduce the heat and simmer for 3 minutes.
5 Slowly drizzle the beaten eggs across the surface of the simmering soup and leave without stirring for 1 minute.
6 Add the soy sauce, vinegar, sesame oil, black pepper and Sichuan pepper, and stir to blend for 1 minute.
7 Stir the cornflour and water again, then pour slowly into the simmering soup while stirring gently, and keep stirring until the soup thickens. Simmer 1 more minute, then turn off the heat.
8 Serve garnished with coriander leaves, ginger and spring onions.

Bamboo shoots are the fresh shoots of the bamboo plant, which make an excellent vegetable. Fresh shoots taste better than canned, but must be peeled, sliced and boiled in water for about 20 minutes before using. Pre-cooked sliced bamboo shoots, packed in water, can be found in the refrigerated section of supermarkets and are convenient and ready to use. Canned bamboo shoots should be boiled for 5 minutes to refresh before using.

For a vegetarian version, use vegetable stock or plain water and double the tofu and black Chinese mushrooms.

Noodles with Sesame Chili Oil

In addition to its delicious taste, this dish delivers a rich parcel of nutritional and medicinal benefits. The sauce contains sesame paste, which is an excellent source of essential fatty acids and benefits bowel functions. Ground peanuts, known in ancient China as "the food of the immortals", provide a quick source of energy, and Sichuan pepper assists digestion and assimilation of nutrients. The recipe below uses ordinary dried wheat noodles that may be purchased in any Asian grocery, but you may also use fresh noodles, as well as rice, buckwheat, egg, or any other type of noodle you wish.

300 g (10 oz) dried wheat noodles
1 teaspoon sesame oil
1 tablespoon coarsely ground roasted peanuts
2 spring onions, finely sliced

Sauce
3 teaspoons sesame paste
165 ml ($^2/_3$ cup) water
3 teaspoons black soy sauce
1 teaspoon sugar
$^1/_2$ teaspoon Sichuan peppercorn powder
2 teaspoons red chili oil
1 teaspoon vinegar

Serves 4
Preparation time: 5 mins
Cooking time: 5 mins

1 To mix the Sauce, place the sesame paste in the bottom of a bowl and slowly pour in the water whilst whisking continuously to blend. Add the soy sauce, sugar and Sichuan pepper, while stirring continuously, then add the chili oil and the vinegar, and blend well.

2 Bring a large pot of water to a boil, add the dried noodles and cook according to the directions on the package.

3 Drain the noodles in a colander, rinse in cold water, drain, place in a large bowl, then drizzle on 1 teaspoon sesame oil and mix well.

4 Add the Sauce to the noodles and toss to mix well, then sprinkle on the ground peanuts and chopped spring onions.

5 Serve in a large serving dish at the table, or distribute equally into individual noodle bowls and serve.

While almost any sort of noodle may be used here, the best choice for both taste and nutrition are freshly made noodles, either from your local market or hand-made in your own kitchen. And if you like the tangy flavor of fresh coriander leaves, it makes a most palatable garnish for this dish. The possibilities are virtually endless!

Peashoots with Garlic and Ginger

500 g (1 lb) fresh Chinese peashoots (*dou miao*—see note)
2 tablespoons oil
3 cloves garlic, minced
2 slices ginger, finely shredded

Sauce
1 teaspoon salt
1 teaspoon sugar
$1/2$ teaspoon Sichuan peppercorn powder
2 teaspoons rice wine
2 teaspoons sesame oil

Serves 4
Preparation time: **5 mins**
Cooking time: **5 mins**

1 Wash the peashoots carefully, and drain well. Remove and discard any wilted or yellowing leaves and tough stalks. Set aside.
2 Combine the Sauce ingredients and set aside.
3 Heat the oil in a wok until hot, add the garlic and ginger and stir-fry quickly to release the aromas, about 30 seconds. Add the peashoots, turning several times to coat evenly with oil, and immediately add the Sauce and continue to stir-fry for about 3 minutes, or until the leaves turn a darker green. Remove to a platter and serve immediately.

Chinese peashoots (*dou miao*) are the delicate leaves at the top of pea plants. They are particularly good when stir-fried simply with a little oil and garlic. Substitute spinach or any other leafy greens.

Spicy Cucumber Salad

500 g (1 lb) small cucumbers, washed
2 teaspoons salt
2 tablespoons finely chopped garlic,
2 red finger-length chilies, deseeded and cut at an angle into thin slices

Dressing
1 tablespoon sugar
$^1/_2$ teaspoon Sichuan peppercorn powder
1 tablespoon apple cider vinegar (or other vinegar)
2 teaspoons sesame oil
$^1/_2$ teaspoon freshly ground black pepper

1 Cut each cucumber in half lengthwise, then cut each half into 3 cm ($1^1/_4$ in) sections crosswise. Place the cucumbers in a bowl, add the salt, toss to coat the pieces evenly, and let stand for 15 minutes. Rinse the cucumbers in cold water to remove the salt, then drain in a colander.
2 Meanwhile, combine the Dressing ingredients, mix well and set aside.
3 Place the drained cucumbers into a serving bowl and add the garlic, chili and Dressing. Stir to blend the flavors. Serve.

Serves 4
Preparation time: 20 mins
Assembling time: 2 mins

Cabbage with Dried Prawns

In Chinese, this dish is called *kai yang bai tsai*, which simply means dried prawns cabbage. It's a very old Sichuan way of cooking cabbage, with the dried prawns serving both a culinary role as a counterpoint to the cabbage, as well as a nutritional role by adding vital minerals from the sea to complement the nutrients contained in the cabbage.

30 g ($^1/_4$ cup) small
  dried prawns
2 tablespoons rice wine
1 medium or large head
  Chinese Cabbage,
  (750 g/1$^1/_2$ lbs—see
  note)
2 tablespoons oil
2 slices ginger, cut in
  thin slivers
2 spring onions, halved
  lengthwise, then cut in
  strips

Sauce
2 teaspoons sesame oil
$^1/_2$ teaspoon freshly
  ground black pepper
1 teaspoon vinegar
1 teaspoon sugar
1 teaspoon salt

Serves 4
Preparation time: 20 mins
Cooking time: 20 mins

1 Place the dried prawns in a small bowl and cover with the rice wine. Leave to soak for 10 to 15 minutes, then drain and set aside.

2 Wash and drain the cabbage. Separate the large leaves, cut each leaf in half lengthwise, then cut each half into smaller pieces. Cut the core into similarly sized pieces. Set both aside to drain.

3 Combine the Sauce ingredients and set aside.

4 Heat the oil in a wok until hot, then add the ginger, spring onions and dried prawns. Stir-fry until their aromas are released, about 2 minutes.

5 Add the cut cabbage and continue to toss until the leaves are coated with oil. Add the sauce and stir to mix well. Cover the wok, lower the heat to medium, and simmer until the cabbage is soft and tender, about 12 to 15 minutes. Check occasionally to see if the cabbage is done, and that it does not get scorched. Remove to a dish and serve hot.

Chinese cabbage has tightly packed white stems and pale green leaves. It has a mild, delicate taste and should only be cooked for a few minutes to retain its color and crunchy texture. Chinese cabbage is a good source of calcium, potassium and iron, and is often eaten in soups. Available year round in supermarkets. This recipe only works well with the long Chinese variety of cabbage, not the round type.

If you are vegetarian, you may replace the dried prawns with pickled turnips, which add an equally distinctive flavor to the dish as the prawn, and which also have their own nutrional benefits.

Sichuan-style Pickled Cabbage

Pickled cabbage dishes, such as the traditional *kimchees* of Korea, are traditional fare throughout Asia, and even Europe has its versions, like the German *sauerkraut*. Pickled cabbage has a wide range of benefits to human health. It contains live enzymes that facilitate digestion of other foods that are eaten with it and it reduces cholesterol. According to Chinese medicine it tones the spleen and stomach, and the chilies, Sichuan peppercorns and other spices in the Sichuan version drive dampness from the body and protect it from parasites and microbes. This dish may be prepared in large and kept in a covered jar in the refrigerator so that you can serve a small side dish of it with your all main meals.

- 3 liters (12 cups) water
- 1 large or 2 small heads of ordinary round white cabbage (not Chinese cabbage), washed and leaves separated (tear large leaves in chunks)
- 6 slices ginger
- 1 large leek, halved lengthwise, then cut in lengths
- 4 red finger-length chilies, halved lengthwise then cut into three sections
- 4 stalks fresh celery, sliced
- 1 medium carrot, cut on angle into slices
- 1 medium daikon, cut on angle into slices

Seasoning
- 10 Sichuan peppercorns
- 750 ml (3 cups) high proof vodka
- 2 teaspoons salt (preferably sea salt)

1 Pour the water into a clean wide-mouthed glass or ceramic vessel that will hold at least 4 liters (16 cups).
2 Add the Seasoning, then the cabbage, then all the remaining ingredients on top of the cabbage. Do not stir. Cover the vessel tightly with a lid (place a weight on top if necessary to keep a tight seal), and set aside to pickle for 3 days.
3 After 3 days, taste to see if it has fermented sufficiently (this depends on climate and season). If ready, serve small dishes of the vegetables with any meal. After 5 days, you should keep the pickled cabbage in the refrigerator, where it will keep for another 7 to 10 days.

This is the basic Sichuan method of preparing pickled cabbage. If you know other ways, such as for Korean kimchee, you may freely mix the various methods to come up with your own favorite combinations. Serving this dish with a meal is particularly beneficial to digestion when there are a lots of meat, poultry and seafood dishes on the table.

Serves 4
Preparation time: 15 mins
Pickling time: 3–5 days

Chinese Greens with Chili and Garlic

1 teaspoon salt
1 teaspoon oil
250 g (8 oz) *Choy Sum* or *Chye Sim* (Chinese Flowering Cabbage), washed and drained (see note)

Sauce
2 tablespoons soy sauce
1 teaspoon sugar
1 teaspoon black soy sauce
1 tablespoon sesame oil
$1/2$ teaspoon Sichuan peppercorn powder
2 red finger-length chilies, seeds removed, finely chopped
2 cloves garlic, minced

1 Mix the Sauce ingredients well and set aside.

2 Bring a large pot of water to a rolling boil, add 1 teaspoon of salt and 1 teaspoon of oil to the water, then add the *choy sum*. When the water has returned to a full boil, remove the *choy sum*, rinse in cold running water to set the color, then drain well.

3 Arrange the cooked *choy sum* on a serving platter, then pour the mixed Sauce evenly on top and serve.

Choy Sum or **Chye Sim**, also known as *Chinese Flowering Cabbage*, is a leafy green vegetable with crisp crunchy stems. Available in supermarkets in Asia, it is now increasingly available in Western countries too. Substitute any other leafy greens.

Serves 4
Preparation time: **10 mins**
Cooking time: **2 mins**

Green Beans with Dried Prawns

3 tablespoons dried prawns, soaked in warm water
125 ml ($^1/_2$ cup) + 2 tablespoons oil
500 g (1 lb) green beans or long beans, tops, tails and strings removed
5 cloves garlic, minced
3 slices ginger, minced
3 spring onions, chopped
1 tablespoon vinegar

Sauce
2 tablespoons rice wine
1 tablespoon water
1 teaspoon salt
1 tablespoon sugar

1 Combine the Sauce ingredients in a small bowl.
2 Drain the dried prawns and chop finely. Set aside.
3 Heat the 125 ml ($^1/_2$ cup) of oil in a wok until hot, add the beans and fry until they begin to crinkle and become soft without burning. Remove and drain, discard the oil.
4 Heat the remaining 2 tablespoons of oil in the wok until hot, add the garlic, ginger, spring onions and prawns and stir-fry for 30 seconds.
5 Add the beans and stir to coat them well in the oil, then add the Sauce, and cook for about 3 minutes.
6 Turn off the heat, stir in the vinegar until blended, then remove to a serving dish.

Serves 4
Preparation time: 12 mins
Cooking time: 10 mins

Eggplant Braised in Fragrant Sauce

This dish makes use of a particular style of Sichuan seasoning that provides a highly aromatic blend of all the basic flavors—sweet, sour, salty, pungent and bitter—in a sauce that has the subtle fragrance of the freshest seafood. To make this dish properly, you should use the long purple Asian eggplant. The traditional method of preparation uses your choice of ground meat, but you may substitute chopped black Chinese mushrooms instead for a vegetarian version, or simply prepare it without meat or mushrooms.

125 ml ($^1/_2$ cup) + 2 tablespoons oil

4 medium Asian eggplants, (about 600 g/1$^1/_2$ lbs), cut in half, then quartered lengthwise (see note)

6 cloves garlic, finely chopped

8 slices ginger, finely chopped

100 g ($^1/_2$ cup) ground pork, beef or lamb

1 tablespoon hot fermented bean paste with chili

6 spring onions, finely chopped

Sauce

2 teaspoons soy sauce

2 teaspoons rice wine

1 teaspoon sesame oil

1 teaspoon vinegar

1 tablespoon sugar, or more to taste

$^1/_2$ teaspoon freshly ground black pepper

1 teaspoon salt

2 tablespoons water

1 Combine the Sauce ingredients and set aside.

2 Heat the 125 ml ($^1/_2$ cup) of oil in a wok until hot, then add the eggplants. Stir-fry, turning frequently, until they change color and soften. Remove the eggplants and set on a rack or colander to drain.

3 Heat the remaining 2 tablespoons of oil until hot. Add the garlic and ginger and stir-fry for 1 minute. Add the ground meat and continue to stir-fry for 2 more minutes. Add the hot fermented bean paste and stir-fry for 30 seconds. Add the Sauce mixture and stir to blend all ingredients.

4 Add the cooked eggplants and stir-fry until evenly coated. Cover, and simmer for 3 to 4 minutes, until tender and fragrant. Remove to a serving dish and sprinkle with chopped spring onions.

Asian eggplants are generally of the slender, purple-skinned variety, 15-20 cm (6-8 in) long. They are mild and need not be salted before use.

To make the vegetarian version, simply substitute **dried black Chinese mushrooms** for the meat. Chopped fresh coriander leaves may be sprinkled on top as well, to accent the flavors.

Serves 4
Preparation time: **15 mins**
Cooking time: **10 mins**

Tofu with Mushrooms and Dried Prawns

Tofu is very popular in Sichuan kitchens because it blends well with the strong seasonings and complex flavors in this cuisine and may be combined with virtually any other ingredients. It is also highly nutritious and economical. In this recipe, tofu is combined with dried black Chinese mushroom, dried prawns, ginger, spring onions and savory seasonings to produce a dish that warms the body, stimulates digestion and serenades the palate.

a250 g (8 oz) *bok choy*, tough leaves discarded (see note)

90 ml ($^1/_3$ cup) + 2 tablespoons oil

2 cakes firm tofu (500 g /1lb), drained, halved then quartered to yield 16 pieces

2 slices ginger, finely sliced

1 spring onion, cut into 3 sections

6 large dried black Chinese mushrooms, soaked in hot water for 20 minutes then drained, tough stems discarded

30 g ($^1/_4$ cup) small dried prawns, soaked in rice wine then drained

60 ml ($^1/_4$ cup) water

2 teaspoons cornflour mixed with 2 tablespoons water

Sauce
2 tablespoons soy sauce
1 teaspoon salt
1 teaspoon sugar
1 tablespoon rice wine
1 teaspoon freshly ground black pepper
1 tablespoon sesame oil

1 Mix the Sauce ingredients and set aside.

2 Blanch the *bok choy* in boiling water for 1 minute, rinse under cold running water, drain, and cut each head in half lengthwise. Set aside.

3 Heat the 90 ml ($^1/_3$ cup) of oil in a wok over high heat until hot but not smoking. Add the tofu pieces and turn gently with a spatula until light golden on all sides. Remove and set on a rack or on paper towels to drain. Discard the oil.

4 Heat the remaining 2 tablespoons of oil in a wok until hot but not smoking. Add the ginger, spring onion, mushrooms and prawns, and stir-fry for 2 minutes. Then add the tofu and continue to stir-fry for another 1 to 2 minutes.

5 Stir the Sauce, then add to the tofu and stir-fry mixture. For more gravy, add the 60 ml ($^1/_4$ cup) of water. Add the cornflour mixture, stir to blend, cover and reduce the heat to medium. Cook for 6 minutes.

6 Separate the *boy choy* leaves and line the edges of a serving dish with them. Transfer the braised tofu onto the dish and serve.

Bok choy is a highly nutritious variety of cabbage with long, crisp stalks and spinach-like leaves. It has a clean, slightly peppery flavor and is a wonderful addition to soups and stir-fries. It is available in most well-stocked supermarkets.

Vegetarians may omit the dried prawns and replace it with finely chopped pickled turnips. Chopped fresh coriander leaves adds a zesty taste as garnish.

Serves 4
Preparation time: 15 mins Cooking time: 20 mins

Hot and Spicy Tofu (Ma Po Tofu)

This is perhaps the single most famous dish of Sichuan. It is said to have been the speciality of an old pock-marked woman in a night market, and that her dish was so renowned that people would travel from all over the province just to taste it. The traditional recipe given below is prepared with ground meat, but an equally tasty vegetarian version may be prepared with finely chopped black Chinese mushrooms.

200 g (1 cup) ground beef, pork or lamb
2 cakes soft tofu (500 g /1 lb), drained
3 tablespoons oil
2 red finger-length chilies, finely chopped
6 cloves garlic, finely chopped
6 slices ginger, finely chopped
1 tablespoon fermented bean paste
1 teaspoon red chili oil or chili paste
4 spring onions, finely chopped
1 teaspoon Sichuan pepper-salt powder

Marinade
1 teaspoon cornflour
$1/_2$ teaspoon sugar
1 teaspoon soy sauce
1 tablespoon rice wine
1 teaspoon sesame oil
$1/_2$ teaspoon Sichuan peppercorn powder

Sauce
250 ml (1 cup) water or chicken stock
1 tablespoon sugar
1 teaspoon salt
1 tablespoon soy sauce
1 teaspoon sesame oil

1 Combine the ground meat and Marinade ingredients in a bowl and set aside. Combine the Sauce ingredients and set aside. Cube the tofu, and finely shop the chilies, garlic and ginger.

2 Heat the oil in a wok over high heat until hot and add the chilies, garlic and ginger and stir-fry for 1 minute. Add the marinated ground meat and continue to stir-fry for 1 more minute. Add the bean paste and chili oil (or chili paste), and cook for 1 more minute.

3 Add the Sauce, stir well to blend, and bring it to a boil. Add the tofu, stirring gently to coat with the Sauce. Cover, reduce heat to medium, and cook for about 8 minutes, stirring occasionally to prevent sticking.

4 Uncover, stir gently to mix, and remove from the heat. Put in a serving bowl and sprinkle with the chopped spring onions and Sichuan pepper-salt powder before serving.

For the vegetarian version, soak 6 to 8 dried black Chinese mushrooms in hot water for 20 minutes. Drain, cut away the tough stems, then cut the caps into small pieces. Set aside on a plate and add in place of meat. Some chefs also like to sprinkle freshly chopped coriander leaves over the dish as a garnish. You may control the heat of the chili flavor by adjusting the amount of red chili oil or paste, and by scraping the seeds and fibers from the fresh chilies for a milder pungency.

Serves 4
Preparation time: **10 mins**   Cooking time: **10 mins**

Pan-fried Fish with Sichuan Spices

Use any deep-water ocean fish for this recipe, such as tuna, swordfish, marlin, shark and salmon. It does not work quite as well with thin fillet-type cuts.

1 large fresh fish steak, about 500 g (1 lb), cleaned and dried
60 g (1 cup) breadcrumbs for frying (specially prepared breadcrumbs for frying are available from Asian stores)
2 tablespoons oil
Chopped spring onions and/or fresh coriander leaves, to garnish

Seasoning
1 teaspoon Sichuan peppercorn powder
1 teaspoon salt
1 teaspoon sugar
$1/2$ teaspoon freshly ground black pepper

1 Mix together all the Seasoning ingredients and place them on a plate. Press both sides of the fish into the Seasoning to absorb them, then leave the fish to marinate for 15 minutes.
2 Coat the fish in the breadcrumbs, pressing the crumbs on to coat the fish well.
3 Heat a flat skillet to medium-hot, then add the oil. Fry the fish until golden brown on both sides, about 4 to 5 minutes for each side. Remove to serving plate.

A nice way to serve it is to line a plate with some chopped iceberg lettuce or some fresh baby spinach, then set the cooked fish steak onto the bed of greens, and top it with your choice of garnish.

Serves 4
Preparation time: 25 mins
Cooking time: 10 mins

Salmon Steamed with Sichuan Seasonings

1 medium carrot,
  quartered lengthwise
2 medium or large
  salmon steaks, about
  500 g (1 lb)
2 tablespoons chopped
  fresh coriander leaves

Sauce
4 cloves garlic, finely
  chopped
6 slices ginger, finely
  chopped
3 spring onions, finely
  chopped
1 red finger-length chili,
  finely chopped
1 tablespoon sesame oil
1 tablespoon oil
1 tablespoon fermented
  bean paste
$1/2$ teaspoon Sichuan
  peppercorn powder
1 teaspoon salt
1 teaspoon sugar
1 teaspoon vinegar
1 tablespoon rice wine

Serves 4
Preparation time: 10 mins
Cooking time: 10 mins

1 Place the four carrot sticks in a heatproof dish that fits into your steamer. Set the salmon steaks onto the carrot sticks (this allows steam to pass under the steaks).

2 To prepare the Sauce, place the minced garlic, ginger, spring onions and chili into a heat-proof bowl. Heat the sesame oil and cooking oil together until they are smoking hot, then pour the hot oil onto the chopped seasonings (it will sizzle a bit). Add all the other Sauce ingredients and mix well with a fork or whisk. Pour the Sauce over the salmon steaks.

3 Bring the water to a boil in the steamer. Set the dish with the salmon steaks and Sauce onto the rack, cover tightly with a lid (place a weight on top to prevent steam from escaping, if necessary), and steam for 8 minutes.

4 Remove the steaming dish with the cooked salmon from the steamer and set it onto a serving dish (do not try to transfer the salmon steaks to a new dish); sprinkle with chopped coriander leaves and serve immediately.

While this recipe works best with salmon, you may also apply it to other types of meaty, deep-water sea fish, such as tuna, swordfish, marlin and so forth. You may also use fillet cuts of virtually any sort of fresh sea fish. Some cooks like to use a sharp knife to cut the steaks into bite-sized pieces in the steaming dish after they come out of the steamer. This makes it easier for diners to serve themselves from the dish using chopsticks.

Fish Braised in Black Bean and Chili

No formal Chinese banquet would be complete without a fresh whole fish prepared in the traditional style of that region. Here is the way Sichuan chefs prepare and cook a whole fresh fish: cooking the fish twice to eliminate any fishy odour and seasoning it with their favorite herbs and a piquant sauce.

1 kg (2 lbs) fresh whole fish, such as sea bass, perch or snapper
Rice wine to rub on fish
Salt to rub on fish
Ginger to rub on wok
375 ml (1¹/₂ cups) oil
4 cloves garlic, sliced
5 slices ginger
1 red finger-length chili, deseeded and chopped
2 spring onions, cut in lengths
1¹/₂ tablespoons fermented bean paste
Fresh coriander leaves, to garnish
Ground black pepper, to taste

Sauce
2 tablespoons rice wine
2 tablespoons soy sauce
2 teaspoons sugar
1 teaspoon vinegar
250 ml (1 cup) chicken stock or water
1 teaspoon cornflour mixed with 2 tablespoons water

Serves 4
Preparation time: **20 mins**
Cooking time: **25 mins**

1 Clean and scale the fish. Score both sides diagonally three times with a sharp knife. Sprinkle the fish inside and outside with rice wine, then rub the inside and outside with salt. Set aside.

2 Mix the Sauce, stir well to blend and set aside.

3 Rub the bottom of a large wok with fresh ginger root, to help prevent sticking. Heat the oil in the wok until medium hot, but not smoking. Using two spatulas, gently place the whole fish into the hot oil and fry until golden brown, about 3 minutes. Jiggle the wok frequently to prevent the fish from sticking to it. Gently turn the fish and fry the other side until golden brown, then carefully remove it from the pan and set aside on paper towels.

4 Pour off all but 60 ml (¹/₄ cup) of the oil and return to medium heat. Add the garlic, ginger, chili and spring onions, and stir-fry for 1 minute. Add the fermented bean paste and continue stir-frying for a further 1 minute. Stir the Sauce again to blend the ingredients, then pour it into the wok, stir to mix, and let it come to a boil.

5 Gently put the fish back into the Sauce, reduce the heat to medium, cover, and braise for about 10 minutes. Turn the fish and braise the other side for 10 minutes, then use two spatulas to carefully remove the fish from the pan and place it on a platter.

6 Pour the remaining Sauce from the pan over the fish, garnish with sprigs of fresh coriander leaves, sprinkle with some coarsely ground black pepper, and serve.

Prawns with Sweet Chili Sauce

Prawns are one of the most popular seafood throughout the world, but no one cooks them better than Chinese chefs. In this Sichuan version, they are marinated in ginger and rice wine, then cooked very quickly with garlic, spring onions and a savory chili sauce. For best results, use fresh prawns but frozen prawns may also be used as long as they are top quality and fresh frozen.

500 g (1 lb) large fresh or frozen raw prawns, peeled and deveined
2 tablespoons oil
4 cloves garlic, chopped
4 spring onions, cut into lengths

Marinade
2 tablespoons rice wine
1 teaspoon sesame oil
1 tablespoon minced ginger
$^{1}/_{2}$ teaspoon sugar

Sauce
2 tablespoons bottled chili sauce
1 teaspoon tomato sauce (ketchup)
$^{1}/_{2}$ teaspoon sugar
1 teaspoon salt
1 teaspoon sesame oil
2 teaspoons cornflour mixed with 125 ml ($^{1}/_{2}$ cup) water

1 Place the prawns in a bowl. Combine the Marinade ingredients, stir, then pour over the prawns, mixing well with a spoon or fingers. Set aside to marinate for 15 to 20 minutes.

2 Combine the Sauce ingredients and set aside.

3 Heat the oil in a wok until hot. Add the garlic and the marinated prawns and stir-fry swiftly until the prawns turn pink and the flesh becomes firm, about 1 to 2 minutes. Add the Sauce and stir-fry for a further 1 minute to mix the ingredients.

4 Add the spring onions and cook for 30 seconds more, then remove to platter and serve immediately.

You may lessen the heat of the chili by using only 1 tablespoon of chili sauce. As with most Sichuan seafood dishes, fresh chopped coriander leaves makes an excellent garnish. You may also apply this recipe to fresh or frozen scallops or fish fillets cut into bite-sized chunks.

Serves 4
Preparation time: 30 mins
Cooking time: 5 mins

Garlic Squid with Celery

This type of dish belongs to a category of homestyle Sichuan cooking known as *xiao chao*, which literally means "small fry", in reference to its simplicity of preparation and humble, albeit highly potent, ingredients. Squid has long been prized in Sichuan family kitchens as an excellent yet inexpensive nutritional source of protein and essential minerals from the sea.

500 g (1 lb) fresh squid
1 tablespoon oil
5–6 cloves garlic, thinly sliced
4 slices ginger
2 red finger-length chilies, cut in pieces
3 spring onions, washed and cut into lengths
5 stalks fresh celery, fibers removed, washed and cut into lengths
Salt to taste

Sauce
2 teaspoons rice wine
1 teaspoon sugar
1 tablespoon sesame oil
1 tablespoon sweet black soy sauce
1 tablespoon water

Serves 4
Preparation time: **15 mins**
  + **2–3 hours soaking time**
Cooking time: **15 mins**

1 Combine the Sauce ingredients and set aside.
2 Remove the tentacles from the squid and cut out the hard beaky portion. Remove the skin from the body of the squid, and clean inside, then cut into bite-sized pieces. Dry thoroughly and set aside.
3 Heat the oil in a wok over medium heat, add the garlic, ginger, and chilies, and stir-fry for about 2 minutes.
4 Increase the heat to high, add the spring onions, celery and squid, and stir-fry for 1 minute. Add the Sauce mixture and continue to stir-fry for another 3 to 4 minutes. Remove to a platter and serve.

Dried scallops can also be used. Simply substitute the scallops for the squid and proceed exactly as above. You may also garnish the finished dish with some chopped fresh coriander leaves, which goes very well with the other seasonings and has a toning effect on the digestive functions of the stomach and spleen.

If **sweet black soy sauce** is not available, add $1/2$ tablespoon brown sugar to 1 tablespoon regular soy sauce.

Gung Bao Squid Braised with Chilies

Gung bao dishes are traditionally attributed to the private kitchen of a certain Duke of Bao in ancient Sichuan, whose personal chef was the reigning master of gourmet cuisine in his time. It involves first scorching dried red chilies in searing hot oil until they are almost black, then tossing in the main ingredients to "explode-fry" (*bao chao*) them quickly in pungent hot oil, and finishing it all off with a savory sauce. This recipe works equally well with chicken chunks or prawns.

1 whole squid (about 500 g/1 lb)
3 tablespoons oil
5 dried red chilies, cut across in thirds
10 Sichuan peppercorns
3 slices ginger, cut in thirds
2 spring onions, cut in thirds

Sauce
1 tablespoon soy sauce
$1/2$ to 1 teaspoons sugar
1 tablespoon rice wine
1 teaspoon tomato sauce (ketchup)
2 teaspoons vinegar
2 teaspoons sesame oil
2 teaspoons cornflour mixed with 125 ml ($1/2$ cup) water

Serves 4
Preparation time: 10 mins
Cooking time: 10 mins

1 Lay the squid flat on a cutting board, and with the point of a sharp knife, make diagonal cuts across the entire surface, cutting only about halfway into the flesh. Repeat same pattern at a 90-degree angle to the first cuts—the result should be a checkerboard of incisions in the flesh, each about 1 cm ($1/2$ in) apart. Then cut the squid into squares or rectangular pieces.
2 Combine the Sauce ingredients and set aside.
3 Bring a pot of water to a rolling boil and add the cut squid. When the water returns to a boil, remove the squid and set aside to drain.
4 Heat the oil in a wok until smoking hot. Add the chilies and let them scorch for 30 to 60 seconds, then add the Sichuan peppercorns, ginger, and spring onions and stir-fry swiftly to release the aromas, about 1 minute.
5 Add the drained squid to the wok and stir-fry quickly for 30 to 60 seconds, then stir the Sauce to mix the ingredients and add to the squid. Stir-fry to blend all flavors for about 3 more minutes, then remove to a platter and serve.

If you like the sharp fresh flavor of coriander leaves, sprinkle some, chopped, onto the finished dish. You may also prepare this recipe with cuttlefish or scallops. The best type of dried chilies for this dish is the medium or large size, which are highly aromatic but not too hot. The smaller the chili, the fiercer its flavor.

Seafood and Mixed Vegetables

This recipe combines a particularly potent blend of fresh seafoods, with strong tonic and warming properties. In order to facilitate digestion, assimilation, and circulation of the proteins, fatty acids, and minerals contained in these items, Sichuan chefs prepare them with seasonings that not only enhance the flavor of the food but also promote its digestion and metabolism.

250 g (8 oz) fresh squid
1 fresh sea cucumber or 100 g (4 oz) fresh prawns or scallops
1 medium carrot
1 medium head broccoli, cut in florets
20 green beans (150 g/5 oz), tops, tails and strings removed, left whole
2 tablespoons oil
1 medium onion, finely sliced
4 cloves garlic, peeled and smashed
1 red finger-length chili, cut diagonally into 3–4 pieces

Sauce
2 tablespoons soy sauce
3 tablespoons rice wine
2 teaspoons sugar
1 tablespoon sesame oil
1$^1/_2$ teaspoons corn-flour mixed with 125 ml ($^1/_2$ cup) water

Serves 4
Preparation time: 25 mins
Cooking time: 10 mins

1 Clean the seafood, then cut them open lengthwise and cut in half. Cut each piece into strips, and place them all into a bowl.

2 Cut the carrot in half lengthwise, then slice each half into semi-circles. Cut florets from the broccoli, peel away any tough skin on the stems, and set aside.

3 Bring a large pot of water to a rolling boil, then place all pre-cut ingredients (seafood, carrot, broccoli, beans) into the boiling water. Poach until the water returns to a full boil, then immediately remove and set aside in a colander to drain.

4 Combine the Sauce and blend well. Set aside.

5 Heat the oil in a wok until smoking hot. Add the onions, garlic and chili and stir-fry swiftly to release their aromas, about 1 minute.

6 Next add all of the pre-cut, poached seafood and vegetables to the wok, and continue to stir-fry until all the ingredients are well coated with oil, about 1 to 2 minutes.

7 Stir the Sauce again to mix, then add to the wok and continue to stir-fry until the Sauce is well blended with the seafood and vegetables, about 2 to 3 more minutes. Remove from the heat, transfer to a platter and serve.

If sea cucumber does not appeal to you, simply substitute another type of seafood, such as scallops or prawns. You may also include some fresh white turnip in this dish, prepared the same way as the carrot, to add extra flavor and color, and to balance the heating properties of this dish with the cooling effect of white turnip.

"Exotic Flavored" Steamed Chicken

The term "exotic flavor" (*guai wei*) refers to a potent combination of spices and seasonings that combines the full spectrum of taste sensations in one harmonious blend. In addition, this blend of herbs provides a stimulating therapeutic boost to the whole system. To prepare this dish, you must first poach a whole chicken the Chinese way. This step takes about $1^1/_2$ hours (but virtually no effort) and may be done well in advance, even the day before.

1 whole chicken ($1^1/_2$ kgs/3 lbs)
250 ml (1 cup) rice wine
3 spring onions, cut into sections
6 slices ginger
1 head iceberg lettuce
Chopped fresh coriander leaves or parsley to garnish

Sauce
8 cloves garlic, finely chopped
8 slices ginger, finely chopped
4 spring onions, finely sliced
1 teaspoon Sichuan peppercorn powder
1 teaspoon salt
1 teaspoon sugar
1 tablespoon sesame oil
1 tablespoon olive oil
$^1/_2$ teaspoon vinegar
2 tablespoons soy sauce
1 tablespoon chili sauce
1 tablespoon sesame paste (or tahini) mixed with 2 tablespoons hot water

1 To poach the chicken, fill a large pot two-thirds full with water, then add the rice wine, spring onions and ginger slices. Bring the water to a rapid boil, then add the whole chicken, breast down. When the water returns to a boil, cover the pot tightly, reduce the heat to low and simmer for 5 minutes. Turn off the heat, wrap the pot well in several towels to keep it hot, then set the chicken aside to poach itself for about $1^1/_2$ hours.

2 When the chicken is done, remove it from the water and set on a rack to drain until ready to use (refrigerate if using the following day).

3 To prepare the Sauce, place the garlic, ginger and spring onions in a heatproof bowl. Add the ground Sichuan pepper, salt and sugar. Heat the sesame and olive oils in a small skillet or wok until smoking hot, then pour over the spices in the bowl and let it sizzle. Add the vinegar, soy sauce, chili sauce and sesame paste, one at a time, stirring each well into the Sauce.

4 Cut the chicken into parts (legs, wings, breast, etc.), then either chop them into bite-sized pieces with a heavy cleaver, or pull the meat from the bones with your fingers.

5 Finely slice the lettuce and arrange it evenly on a large serving platter. Arrange the chicken meat neatly on top, then pour or spoon the sauce evenly over the chicken. Garnish with fresh coriander leaves or parsley before serving.

Serves 4
Preparation time: 2 hours   Assembling time: 15 mins

Chili Chicken with Peanuts

Chili and chicken is one of the all-time great culinary combinations, and virtually every Asian culture has its various versions of this dynamic duo. In Sichuan cuisine, there are at least a dozen major variations on this theme. This one is for those whose palates enjoy a really potent pungency in their food. For a hotter taste, keep the seeds and fibers; for milder taste, remove them first.

3 fresh chicken legs (about 750 g/1$^1/_2$ lbs), including thighs and drumsticks
2 tablespoons oil
8 cloves garlic, finely chopped
3 red finger-length chilies, finely chopped
50 g ($^1/_3$ cup) skinned roasted peanuts
2 spring onions, cut in thirds

Marinade
1 teaspoon soy sauce
$^1/_2$ teaspoon cornflour
1 teaspoon rice wine

Sauce
2 tablespoons hot fermented bean paste
1 teaspoon sugar, or more to taste
1 teaspoon soy sauce
$^1/_2$ teaspoon vinegar
2 teaspoons sesame oil
1 teaspoon cornflour mixed with 125 ml ($^1/_2$ cup) water

1 Debone the chicken legs, then cut the meat into chunks. Mix the Marinade and cover the chicken with it. Leave aside to marinate for about 15 minutes.
2 Combine the Sauce ingredients and set aside.
3 Heat the oil in a wok until hot. Add the chopped garlic and chili and stir-fry quickly for 30 seconds, then add the marinated chicken and continue to stir-fry until the meat turns color and gets firm, about 3 to 4 minutes. Add the peanuts and spring onions and stir.
4 Stir the Sauce again to mix the ingredients, then pour over the chicken and stir to coat well. Cover, reduce the heat to medium, and simmer for about 3 minutes. Remove to a serving dish.

Fresh or frozen green peas add color and flavor to this dish, and may be added along with, or instead of, the peanuts. You may adjust the intensity of the flavor by keeping or removing the seeds and fibers of the chilies, and also adjusting the amount of hot fermented bean paste used in the sauce. Either chopped fresh coriander leaves, or chopped Western parsley, makes a good garnish, and you may also sprinkle the finished dish lightly with a bit of Sichuan pepper-salt powder to add further dimension to the hot flavors.

Serves 4
Preparation time: 20 mins
Cooking time: 10 mins

Minced Chicken in a Pumpkin

The recipe calls for chopping the chicken into bite-sized chunks, including the bone, but if you prefer using deboned chicken, that's fine too. The pumpkin flesh inside may also be scooped out and eaten along with the chicken.

1 whole fresh pumpkin, (about 1$^1/_2$ kgs/3 lbs)
1 kg (2 lbs) fresh chicken (with bone), or 750 g (1$^1/_2$ lbs) boneless chicken
300 g (1$^1/_2$ cups) uncooked white or brown rice (see note)
2 tablespoons Sichuan peppercorns
4 slices ginger, shredded
3 spring onions, cut into lengths

Marinade
2 teaspoons soy sauce
2 teaspoons sesame oil
1 tablespoon sugar
2 tablespoons rice wine
1 teaspoon fermented bean paste
1 teaspoon cornflour mixed with 1 tablespoon water

Serves 4
Preparation time: 35 mins
Cooking time: 1 hour

1 Cut the top off the pumpkin and scrape out the seeds and fibers with a spoon, rinse and set aside.
2 With a large cleaver, chop the chicken through the bone into bite-sized pieces, or cut the boneless chicken into similar sized pieces. Mix the Marinade, add to the chicken and mix well with your fingers, then set aside to marinate for 20 to 30 minutes.
3 In a dry wok, toast the rice and the Sichuan peppercorns until they are golden brown and aromatic. Transfer to a mortar and grind to a coarse powder, or use an electric grinder.
4 Roll each piece of marinated chicken in the spicy rice powder until well coated, then place inside the pumpkin. Add the ginger and spring onions to the pumpkin along with the chicken, distributing evenly; pour any extra marinade into the pumpkin.
5 Pour the water into a very large pot or wok to a height of about 4 to 8 cm (1$^1/_2$ to 3 in), place a steaming rack inside and bring the water to a boil.
6 Place the pumpkin on a pie plate, or other heat-proof dish, and set it carefully on the rack in the steamer. Cover with a tight lid (add a weight on top of the lid if necessary to seal it), and let the pumpkin steam for about 1 hour. If the water runs dry, pour in another cup or two.
7 When cooked, carefully remove the pumpkin from the steamer, and set on the table to serve. If you have trouble getting it out of the steamer, simply scoop out individual servings directly from the steamer.

Brown rice is rice with its golden-brown bran intact. It has a nutty texture and more fiber than milled white rice, and requires more water as well as longer cooking time.

Gung Bao Chicken with Dried Chilies

This is another variation of the *gung bao* style of cooking, using chicken and a slightly different blend of seasonings. The basic method involves stir-frying the main ingredient in very hot oil in which dried chilies have been scorched, but you may adjust the sauce ingredients to suit your own tastes, and try different combinations from time to time.

500 g (1 lb) boned fresh chicken, cut in chunks
2 tablespoons oil
5 dried red chilies, deseeded and cut in thirds
5 to 8 Sichuan peppercorns
3 cloves garlic, coarsely chopped
6 slices ginger
3 spring onions, cut into lengths

Marinade
1 tablespoon rice wine
1 teaspoon soy sauce
1 teaspoon sesame oil
$1/2$ teaspoon sugar, or more to taste
$1/2$ teaspoon cornflour mixed with 4 tablespoons water

Sauce
3 tablespoons sweet black soy sauce
1 teaspoon vinegar
1 tablespoon rice wine
1 teaspoon sesame oil
1 teaspoon salt
1 teaspoon cornflour mixed with 4 tablespoons water

1 Place the chicken chunks in a bowl and cover with the Marinade ingredients. Mix well with your fingers and set aside to marinate for 15 to 20 minutes.
2 Combine the Sauce ingredients and set aside.
3 Heat the oil in a wok over high heat until hot, add the cut dried chilies, and scorch for 30 to 60 seconds. Add the Sichuan peppercorns, garlic and ginger, and stir-fry for 30 seconds more.
4 Add the marinated chicken and stir-fry quickly, until the chicken changes color and gets firm, about 4 minutes. Add the sauce, stir to blend all the ingredients, cover, reduce heat to medium, and braise for 5 minutes. Uncover, add the spring onions, stir to mix with the chicken for 30 seconds, then remove to a serving dish.

If you don't like biting into the whole Sichuan peppercorns in the dish, omit them and sprinkle the finished dish with Sichuan pepper-salt powder instead. Add about $1/2$ cup of fresh or frozen green peas after stir-frying the chicken, but before adding the sauce. As with most Sichuan food, chopped fresh coriander leaves makes a refreshing garnish. If sweet black soy sauce is not available, substitute with 3 tablespoons regular dark or light soy sauce mixed with 2 teaspoons brown sugar.

Serves 4
Preparation time: **30 mins**
Cooking time: **15 mins**

Five Spice Fried Chicken

This is one of the more renowned dishes from Sichuan, popular throughout China. It utilizes no fermented seasonings whatsoever, such as soy sauce or vinegar, relying entirely on the five flavors contained in the five spice powder. This permits the full flavor of the chicken to emerge, enhanced by the spices but not masked or altered by fermented products. For best results, and for optimum nutrition, it's best to use only free-range chickens.

12 chicken drumsticks
2 tablespoons five spice powder (see note)
250 ml (1 cup) oil
1 bunch fresh parsley, washed and drained
2^1/$_2$ tablespoons Sichuan pepper-salt powder
Chopped fresh coriander leaves and/or spring onions, to garnish

Serves 4
Preparation time: **1 hour**
Cooking time: **15 mins**

1 Wash the drumsticks and pat dry with paper towels; roll them in the five spice powder until evenly coated and set aside to marinate for 1 hour.

2 Heat the oil in a wok until hot, but not smoking. Add the marinated drumsticks to the hot oil and fry until golden brown, turning occasionally for even cooking, about 8 to 10 minutes depending on thickness of the drumsticks. Remove and set on a rack to drain.

3 In the remaining hot oil, fry the fresh parsley sprigs until crispy, about 1 minute; remove and drain.

4 Arrange the cooked parsley sprigs around the edge of a large serving dish, then place the fried drumsticks in the center. Sprinkle evenly with the Sichuan pepper-salt powder, garnish with the coriander leaves and/or spring onions, and serve.

This is a popular *xia jiu cai* in China, which means a dish to help get the liquor down. It is often served as a bar snack and is just as popular with children, which makes it a good choice for family meals.

Five spice powder is a highly aromatic blend of Sichuan pepper, cinnamon bark, clove, fennel and star anise, ground to a fine powder and used to season stir-fried noodles, in marinades and for sauces.

Braised Chicken Chunks

This is a style of chicken native to Chengdu, the provincial capital of Sichuan. Like so many Sichuan dishes, the chicken here is cooked twice, first by deep-frying, then by braising with seasonings. The braising stage of the process removes much of the oil that clings to the chicken after deep-frying, thereby making the dish far less heavy and far more easy to digest, while still retaining the crisp texture imparted by the initial frying.

3 whole chicken legs,
 (about 750 g/1$^1/_2$ lbs)
375 ml (1$^1/_2$ cups) oil
 for deep-frying
3 tablespoons oil for stir-
 frying
3 cloves garlic, finely
 chopped
5 slices ginger, finely
 chopped
10 Sichuan peppercorns
375 ml (1$^1/_2$ cups) water
2 stalks fresh celery,
 strings removed, diced

Sauce
1 tablespoon fermented
 bean paste
1 teaspoon sugar
2 teaspoons rice wine
2 teaspoons sesame oil
2 teaspoons cornflour
 mixed with 2 table-
 spoons water

1 Debone the chicken legs, then cut the meat into chunks. Heat the 375 ml (1$^1/_2$ cups) of oil until hot, then add the chicken chunks and deep-fry until golden. Remove from the oil and drain on a wire rack or paper towels.

2 Combine the Sauce ingredients and set aside.

3 Heat 3 tablespoons of oil until hot, but not smoking. Add the garlic, ginger and Sichuan peppercorns and stir-fry swiftly to release the aromas, about 30 seconds.

4 Add the chicken to the oil, stir-fry for 1 minute, then add the Sauce. Stir to blend all flavors, then add the water, and stir until it returns to a boil. Lower the heat to medium, cover, and braise slowly until most of the fluid has evaporated, leaving the chicken bubbling in a thick sauce.

5 Transfer to a serving dish, sprinkle the celery evenly over the top, and serve.

You may also try this recipe with fresh fish, preferably fish such as tuna, swordfish, marlin, etc. Prepare the fish in the same way as chicken, but reduce the cooking times a little. Chopped spring onions and/or chopped fresh coriander leaves also go very well as garnish for this recipe.

Serves 4
Preparation time: 20 mins
Cooking time: 5 mins

Shredded Chicken with Sesame and Chili

Often referred to in the English versions of Chinese menus as Bon Bon Chicken, presumably because it's pronounced *bang bang ji* in Chinese, this is one of the most popular chicken concoctions in Sichuan. The term *bang bang* is equivalent to the English word drumstick as a vernacular reference to the leg of the chicken. This dish is usually served as a cold appetizer at the beginning of a meal, but it may also be the main event in a simple lunch.

2 large chicken legs, about 500 g (1 lb)
$^1/_2$ head iceberg lettuce, or other head lettuce, finely shredded
1 red bell pepper, cut in thin strips
$^1/_2$ teaspoon sea salt
1 teaspoon sesame oil

Sauce
$2^1/_2$ tablespoons dark Chinese sesame paste or tahini
60 ml ($^1/_4$ cup) chicken stock or water
$^1/_2$ teaspoon Sichuan peppercorn powder
2 teaspoons sugar
1 teaspoon vinegar
1 teaspoon red chili oil
2 teaspoons sesame oil
2 teaspoons black soy sauce
$^1/_2$ teaspoon salt
1 tablespoon freshly grated ginger
1 tablespoon finely chopped garlic

Serves 4
Preparation time: 20 mins
Cooking time: **1 hour**

1 Poach the chicken legs by placing them in a large pot with sufficient water to cover them by 3 cm ($1^1/_4$ in) and bring to a boil. Reduce the heat, cover tightly, and simmer for 10 minutes. Turn off the heat, and set aside to poach in hot water for 30 minutes. Remove the chicken from the water and drain.

2 Spread the lettuce evenly on a serving plate. Place the strips of red bell pepper into a bowl with the sea salt, and mix well with your fingers to soften them. Add 1 teaspoon of sesame oil and continue to mix with your fingers until coated, then arrange the strips evenly over the shredded lettuce.

3 Mix the Sauce by blending the sesame paste, or tahini, with the water in a bowl. Add the ground Sichuan pepper and mix well, then add the remaining ingredients, one at a time, stirring continuously with a whisk or fork, until well blended.

4 Remove the skin from the poached chicken and pull the meat from the bones. Tear the meat into fine shreds and pile the shredded chicken on top of the lettuce and bell peppers. Drizzle the Sauce evenly over the chicken and serve.

This dish may be garnished with chopped fresh coriander leaves or shredded spring onions. You may also use other parts of the chicken, particularly if you wish to prepare a bigger portion. For example, you may poach a whole chicken and shred the entire chicken to make a larger serving. To poach a whole chicken, follow the instructions for Exotic Flavored Chicken on page 42.

Fragrant Crispy Plump Duck

Duck is an excellent tonic food for the autumn and winter seasons, and is particularly renowned for its potent restorative benefits to the kidney energy system, which is a primary source of human vitality. This distinctive method of preparation, which involves steaming the whole duck first, then frying it, seals in the duck's essential flavors and nutrients on the inside and produces a delicious crispy skin on the outside. You will receive praise for your cooking whenever you present this dish to a table of hungry diners.

2 teaspoons salt

2 teaspoons Sichuan peppercorns

1 teaspoon black peppercorns

4 spring onions, finely chopped

3 slices ginger, finely chopped

1 tablespoon rice wine

1 whole duck, about (about 2 kgs/4 lbs), cleaned

6 pieces star anise (see note)

15 g ($^1/_3$ cup) chopped coriander leaves

Serves 4
Preparation time: 10 mins
Cooking time: 10 mins

Star Anise is a dried brown flower with 8 woody petals, each with a shiny seed inside, which gives a flavor of cinnamon and aniseed. Use whole and remove from the dish before serving.

1 Heat a dry wok over medium flame, then add the salt and the Sichuan and black peppercorns, and stir continuously for 1 to 2 minutes, until the peppercorns are fragrant. Pour into a mortar and grind to a coarse powder.

2 In a bowl, mix the salt and pepper powder with the spring onions, ginger and rice wine and mix well. Rub this mixture all over the duck, inside and out. Place the star anise and any remaining mixture inside the duck's abdominal cavity. Place the duck on a dish, cover with cellophane wrap, and leave aside to marinate for 2 to 3 hours.

3 Set a steaming rack in a pot or wok large enough to hold the whole duck. Bring some water to a boil, then place the duck on a heat-proof dish and set it on the rack in the steamer. Cover tightly, and steam the duck for $1^1/_2$ hours, making sure to replenish the water from time to time.

4 Remove the duck and leave aside on a rack to cool.

5 Pour enough oil into a large wok to fill it about $^1/_3$ full (about $1^1/_2$ to 2 liters, or 6 to 8 cups of oil). Heat until smoking hot, then reduce the flame slightly and very carefully immerse the whole duck into the hot oil, breast side down, covering the duck completely in oil if possible, and deep-fry for 3 to 4 minutes, until the skin turns a rich golden brown. If the duck is not fully immersed in oil, turn and fry the other side for 2 more minutes. Remove the duck from the oil and drain on a rack.

6 Place the duck on a chopping board, cut in half, separate the legs and wings. Using a Chinese cleaver, chop all pieces into chunks. Arrange the chopped duck on a platter and garnish with coriander leaves. Serve.

Sliced Pork with Garlic Sauce

This is a classic Sichuan dish and is very easy to prepare. The pork itself is cooked in a particular two-step method which gives the meat a special resilient texture, while at the same time eliminating any rank taste. Sichuan cooks pay close attention to the textures as well as the tastes of the foods they prepare for the table, because the texture of food, and how it feels in the mouth when chewed, has always been regarded as a very important consideration in Chinese cuisine.

500 g (1 lb) fresh belly
   pork or pork loin

Sauce
2 tablespoons black soy
   sauce
2 teaspoons sugar
2 teaspoons sesame oil
1 teaspoon red chili oil
1 teaspoon salt
2 teaspoons water
8–10 cloves garlic, finely
   minced

Serves 4
Preparation time: **30 mins**
Cooking time: **10 mins**

1 Bring a large pot of water to a rolling boil. Add the whole piece of pork, let the water return to a boil, reduce the heat to medium, simmer, and boil until thoroughly cooked (about 25 minutes). Remove the meat and set aside to drain and cool; keep the water simmering.

2 Combine the Sauce ingredients and stir well to blend the flavors. Set aside.

3 Place the pork on a cutting board. Using a very sharp knife, cut the pork into very thin slices. If the meat has a layer of fat, it should be cut so that each slice has a bit of fat attached.

4 Bring the pot of water back to a full boil and gently add the sliced pork to re-heat and further set the texture, then remove immediately to a colander and drain.

5 Arrange the hot sliced pork on a platter, then pour the sauce evenly over the meat. Serve.

Black soy sauce gives the sauce a thick texture and has enough body to balance the strong ration of garlic. You may garnish this dish with some chopped fresh coriander leaves to give it additional color and flavor.

Twice-cooked Pork (Hui Guo Rou)

In this recipe, the pork is first pre-cooked in boiling water, as in the previous recipe, to eliminate any rank flavor from the meat and render out some of the fat. It is then finely sliced and cooked again by stir-frying with Sichuan seasonings and a savory sauce. The distinctive taste of this dish is created primarily by two ingredients in the sauce: fermented bean paste (*dou ban jiang*) and sweet bean paste (*tien mien jiang*). The former is a highly aromatic, pungent ferment of soya beans, while the latter is soya bean ferment to which sugar and other ingredients have been added to produce a sweet tasting paste.

500 g (1 lb) fresh belly pork or pork loin
6 large leeks, washed
2 tablespoons oil
6 thin slices ginger
1 green and 1 red bell pepper cut in squares
1 red finger-length chili, deseeded and cut in 3-4 pieces

Sauce
1 tablespoon fermented bean paste
2 teaspoons sweet fermented bean paste
2 teaspoons sugar
2 teaspoons rice wine
1 tablespoon soy sauce
1 tablespoon water

Serves 4
Preparation time: **30 mins**
Cooking time: **10 min**

1 Cook the pork in boiling water as described in Step 1 on page 58 and discard the water. Cut the pork across the grain into wafer-thin slices. If using a fatty cut, slice it so that there is a strip of fat on each piece.
2 Wash the leeks well, cut off and discard the top of the green leaves, keeping just the white stalk and the tender portion of the green part. Cut each stalk in half lengthwise, and then slice them into sections.
3 Combine the Sauce ingredients and set aside.
4 Heat 1 tablespoon of the oil in a wok until hot. Add the ginger, green and red bell peppers and red chili and stir-fry swiftly for 1 minute, then add the leeks and continue stir-frying for one minute more. Remove from the wok and set aside on a plate.
5 Add the remaining 1 tablespoon of oil to the wok, and when hot, add the sliced pork and stir-fry quickly for 1 to 2 minutes, until the pork is slightly seared around the edges.
6 Add the fried leeks, ginger and peppers. Stir to mix, then immediately add the Sauce, stir to blend, and let simmer for about 3 minutes over medium heat. Remove to a platter and serve.

If you prefer a hotter chili flavor, add 1 to 2 teaspoons red chili oil to the sauce, or substitute several hot dried chilies for the one fresh chili, or substitute 2 teaspoons of good quality chili sauce for the sweet bean paste. Of the two fermented bean pastes, only the pungent one is essential to the success of the dish, so if you cannot find the sweet bean paste, simply omit it from the recipe.

Lamb with Piquant Sauce

Among the common domestic meats—beef, pork and lamb—lamb is by far the most beneficial to human health. Lamb fat contains a nutrient called l-carnitine, which carries fat out of the liver and feeds it to the heart as fuel. Pork and beef fat, however, are very difficult to digest and can cause liver congestion. While some people complain that lamb has a strong taste, this is completely eliminated by the marinating process, as well as the aromatic seasonings used to cook it in this recipe. Nevertheless, this recipe may be also be applied with equal success to beef and pork, as well as chicken.

500 g (1 lb) lamb loin
4 spring onions, cut in half lengthwise, then shredded
3 tablespoon oil

Marinade
1 teaspoon cornflour mixed with 1 tablespoon of water
1 tablespoon soy sauce
1 egg white
$1/2$ teaspoon sugar

Sauce
1 tablespoon sweet fermented bean paste
1 teaspoon sugar
1 teaspoon salt
2 teaspoons rice wine
1 tablespoon Sichuan peppercorn powder
1 tablespoon sesame oil
2 tablespoons bottled chili sauce

Serves 4
Preparation time: **15 mins**
Cooking time: **10 mins**

1 Cut the lamb into thin slices, then cut the slices into fine strips and place in a bowl.
2 To make the Marinade, combine the ingredients, then pour over the lamb and set aside for 15 minutes.
3 Spread the shredded spring onions evenly onto a serving plate and set aside.
4 Combine the Sauce ingredients and set aside.
5 Heat the 2 tablespoons of oil in a wok over high heat until hot. Add the marinated lamb and stir-fry swiftly for about 4 minutes. Remove the lamb to a plate and set aside. Discard the oil.
6 Heat the remaining 1 tablespoon of oil in the wok and when hot, add the Sauce mixture and stir-fry for about 1 minute.
7 Return the lamb to the wok and cook for another 3 to 4 minutes. Remove the lamb and place on top of the shredded spring onions on the serving dish.

For a bit of extra **ma la** taste, you may sprinkle some Sichuan pepper-salt powder on top of the finished dish. A garnish of chopped fresh coriander leaves and or chopped fresh chili also goes well with this dish. Instead of spring onions you can also used finely sliced onions or mung bean sprouts as a bed for the cooked lamb. If using pork,increase the cooking time to 6 minutes for the pre-cooking, and 6 minutes for the final cooking. This is also an excellent way to prepare venison, wild boar and other wild game meats.

Index